THE NATIONAL POETRY SERIES

The National Poetry Series was established in 1978 to publish five collections of poetry annually through five participating publishers. The manuscripts are selected by five poets of national reputation. Publication is funded by the Copernicus Society of America, James A. Michener, Edward J. Piszek, the Mobil Foundation, the National Endowment for the Arts, the Friends of the National Poetry Series, and the five publishers—E. P. Dutton, Graywolf Press, William Morrow and Company, Persea Books, and the University of Illinois Press.

The National Poetry Series, 1987

Junk City
   Barbara Anderson
   Selected by Robert Pinsky/Persea Books
Cardinals in the Ice Age
   John Engels
   Selected by Philip Levine/Graywolf Press
Little Star
   Mark Halliday
   Selected by Heather McHugh/William Morrow
Cities in Motion
   Sylvia Moss
   Selected by Derek Walcott/University of Illinois Press
Red Roads
   Charlie Smith   ·
   Selected by Stanley Kunitz/E. P. Dutton

LITTLE STAR

POEMS BY

LITTLE STAR

MARK HALLIDAY

WILLIAM MORROW AND COMPANY, INC.
NEW YORK

Library of Congress Cataloging-in-Publication Data

Halliday, Mark, 1949–
   Little star.
   (National poetry series)
   I. Title. II. Series.
PS3558.A386L5   1987   811'.54   87-11234
ISBN 0-688-07519-3
ISBN 0-688-07530-4 (pbk.)

Printed in the United States of America

First Edition

1 2 3 4 5 6 7 8 9 10

BOOK DESIGN BY DALE COTTON

Some of the poems in *Little Star* have appeared in periodicals, as follows: "Get It Again," "Key to the Highway," "The Students," "Work," and "New York Breeze" appeared in *The New Republic*. "Why the HG Is Holy" appeared in *Michigan Quarterly Review*. "Describers," "Western North Carolina," and "Functional Poem" appeared in *Ploughshares*.
"Casualty Report" reprinted from *The Massachusetts Review*. Copyright © 1982, *The Massachusetts Review*, Inc.
"Little Star" appeared in *Against Our Vanishing: Winter Conversations on Poetry and Poetics* by Allen Grossman and Mark Halliday (Boston: Rowan Tree Press, 1981).

Quotations in certain of the poems are made from the following sources: "Ask Me Why," page 21: "Ask Me Why," copyright © 1963 by John Lennon and Paul McCartney, Dick James Music Ltd., London/Concertone Songs Inc., released on the album *The Early Beatles* (Capitol).
"Blind Date," page 25: "Wouldn't It Be Nice," lyrics copyright © 1966 by Tony Asher and Brian Wilson, Irving Music Inc., released on the album *Pet Sounds* by the Beach Boys (Capitol).
"Describers," page 38: from the novel *The Waves*, by Virginia Woolf (London: Hogarth Press, 1931; New York: Harcourt, Brace, 1931).
"New York Breeze," page 49: "Meditation Mama," copyright © 1966 by John Phillips, Wingate Music Corp., released on the album *The Papas and the Mamas*, by the Mamas and the Papas (Dunhill).

Thanks to Frank Bidart; and Annie Carter, Bob Dylan, Allen Grossman, Beverley Cline Halliday, E. M. Halliday, Kim Halliday, Vito Picone, Robert Pinsky, Norman Rosten, Lloyd Schwartz, Bruce Springsteen, Kate Stearns, Ronald Thomas.

CONTENTS

LITTLE STAR

GET IT AGAIN

In 1978 I write something about how
happiness and sorrow are intertwined
and I feel good, insightful, and it seems
this reflects some healthy growth of spirit,
some deep maturation—then
I leaf through an eleven-year-old notebook
and spot some paragraphs I wrote in 1967
on Keats's "Ode on Melancholy" which
seem to say some of it better, or
almost better, or as well though differently—
and the waves roll out, and the waves roll in.

In 1972 I often ate rye toast with peanut butter,
the toast on a blue saucer beside my typewriter,
I took huge bites between paragraphs about love and change;
today it's a green saucer, cream cheese, French bread,
but the motions are the same and in a month or so
when the air is colder I'll be back to my autumn snack,
rye toast with peanut butter, an all-star since '72. . . .
I turned around on sidewalks to stare at women's asses
plenty of times in the sixties and
what do you think will be different in the eighties?
In 1970, mourning an ended love, I listened
to a sailor's song with a timeless refrain,
and felt better—that taste of transcendence
in the night air
and

and here it is in 1978, the night air, hello.

My journalist friend explains the challenge
of his new TV job: you work for a week
to get together one 5-minute feature,

and then
it's gone—
vanished into gray-and-white memory,
a fading choreography of electric dots—
and you're starting it all over,
every week that awesome energy demand:
to start over

In 1973 I played hundreds of games of catch
with a five-year-old boy named Brian.
Brian had trouble counting so we practiced
by counting the times we tossed the ball
without missing. When Brian missed
he was on the verge of despair for a moment
but I taught him to say
"Back to zero!" to give him a sense of
always another chance. I tried to make it sound
exciting to go back to zero, and eventually
our tone was exultant when we shouted in unison
after a bad toss or fumble
back to zero.

In 1977 I wrote a poem called "Repetition Rider"
and last winter I revised it three times
and I thought it was finished.

"It's not like writing," says my journalist friend,
"where your work is permanent—no matter how obscure,
written work is durable. . . . That's why
it can grow—you can move beyond
what you've already said."

Somewhere I read or heard something good
about what Shakespeare meant in *Lear*
when he wrote: "Ripeness is all."
I hope it comes back to me.

I see myself riding
the San Francisco subway in 1974
scrawling something in my little red notebook
about "getting nowhere fast".
I see Brian's big brown eyes lit
with the adventure of starting over
and oblivious, for a moment,
of the extent to which he is
doomed by his disabilities.
And the waves
roll out, and the waves roll in.
This poem

could go on a long time,
but you've already understood it;
you got the point some time ago,

and you'll get it again

KEY TO THE HIGHWAY

I remember riding somewhere in a fast car
with my brother and his friend Jack Brooks
and we were listening to *Layla & Other Love Songs*
by Derek & the Dominos. The night was dark,
dark all along the highway. Jack Brooks was
a pretty funny guy, and I was delighted
by the comradely interplay between him and my brother,
but I tried not to show it for fear of inhibiting them.
I tried to be reserved and maintain a certain
dignity appropriate to my age, older by four years.
They knew the Dominos album well having played the cassette
many times, and they knew how much they liked it.
As we rode on in the dark I felt the music was,
after all, wonderful, and I said so
with as much dignity as possible. "That's right,"
said my brother. "You're getting smarter," said Jack.
We were listening to "Bell Bottom Blues"
at that moment. Later we were listening to
"Key to the Highway", and I remember how
my brother said, "Yeah, yeah." And Jack sang
one of the lines in a way that made me laugh.
I am upset by the fact that that night is so absolutely gone.
No, "upset" is too strong. Or is it.
But that night is so obscure—until now
I may not have thought of that ride once
in eight years—and this obscurity troubles me.
Death is going to defeat us all so easily.
Jack Brooks is in Florida, I believe,
and I may never see him again, which is
more or less all right with me; he and my brother
lost touch some years ago. I wonder
where we were going that night. I don't know;
but it seemed as if we had the key to the highway.

CASUALTY REPORT

My little notebook with the battle of Bunker Hill on the cover—
how can I make you care about it?

I bought it early in 1976 to help me
hang on to everything
in my head. Thoughts, questions, lists, quotations,
doggerel, free and forced associations—
all inscribed
in neat print
with nothing misspelled and nothing scratched out;

there is one essay that filled at least seven of the small pages
advising me on how to love Annie—
jealousy and self-doubt were twisting me in yellow knots
while an uncomfortable mystery resided in the experience of
going to Compo Beach with Annie in 1976
ten years after our high school graduation—Compo,
where women's bodies had troubled me so many times,
scene of a hundred imagined defeats whose vivid memory made it
almost appalling that now, with her, there could be
ordinary days at the beach (as if time were *not* desperately
      poignant)—
I pondered all this in the essay; it's all there
in the notebook.

On a hot day that summer I sat
in Dante's Inferno, a cheap restaurant next to the laundromat
of South Windsor, Connecticut, eating a bedraggled dessert
and writing (my hand sweating on the Bic)
a blistering parody of the plotty plot of
one of Iris Murdoch's long love-tangle novels.
I'm pretty sure that's in the notebook. I'm
really almost positive.

■ 17

In September I took a teaching job in Syracuse,
had to move away from Annie, and I'm sure
the notebook contains several witty verses and aphorisms
about the bleakness of Syracuse. . . .
There was a lot of snow that year, and it became
an inescapable metaphor.

Also I have a sense that a sexual fantasy of some kind
made its way boldly onto the last pages of the notebook—
I can't remember, but I have a nervous feeling
(my name was on the first page)—
and there was other stuff, and some of it
could have mattered in a lasting way
to me—

I left this Bunker Hill notebook
on the shelf of a pay phone
in the Syracuse bus station
one snowy night. (It had phone numbers in it too.)
Realizing my loss the next day I went back
and they did have a Lost & Found box
and my heart leapt
but it wasn't there. It's
gone.
        (Actually, it *could* have been the Battle of Trenton;
        or Brandywine?
        Definitely a Revolutionary War battle, in any case . . .)

Inevitability of loss,
disappearance of temporary versions of the self,
neurotic dependence on defensive reportage,
the way language about language is apt to be frustrating,
the way most old personal talismans are nontransferable
        (because not fully retrieved?)—

18

yes, all that, but still

what I want you to come away with (because
if you *will* take it, I get it back) is this:

my small 1976 notebook
with a heroic battle scene on the cover.
Make a place for it in the permanence of acknowledgment
and I can stop missing it, can feel I've signed
another truce in the endless war with the past.

ASK ME WHY

Beauty too rich for use,
for earth too dear!
—*Romeo and Juliet*

A certain spring evening in my sophomore year comes back to
   me
with a sad sweetness—the evening when Richard met Ann.
Richard was sort of my best friend. Ann was Cathy's best friend.
Cathy and I were lovers, since freshman year.
I guess it was coincidence that Ann and Richard had arrived
from their respective universities to visit us at ours
on the same day.
My memory starts when the four of us returned to
   David's large room
in Slater Hall after dinner. (David, a mutual friend
with the largest room, was away somewhere.)
We sprawled on the selfless dormitory furniture wondering
what to do and what was up. . . . It was
that Richard and Ann might be falling in love.

Falling in love: we held this possibility
gently among us with our forty fingertips,
all four of us anxious to keep it alive
without having judged whether it was really a good idea,
wanting a dreamy romance to grow before our eyes
while dusk thickened outside the old brick dorm.

Twenty years old, we already knew enough to know
that true love doesn't just blossom in front of you,
especially not when you're expecting it and trying to
   nurse it along,
love is like a clock, it moves only when you're looking
   away. . . .
We *weren't* old enough to doubt it exists at all.

■ 20

We talked about professors, the Chicago conspiracy trial,
Tennessee Williams, hopes for summer travel, François Truffaut.
We played cards. In an odd way we were bored; our talk
   dwindled;
Richard put on *The Early Beatles*
and we sat around vaguely and softly singing along
in David's large room dark now.
It had become evident that we were not going to a movie
or the library or anywhere. I was afraid to suggest anything
that might make me guilty of breaking the magic mood.
Richard played both sides of *The Early Beatles* at least twice,
and we all got the point: the point was that at twenty
we could already be nostalgic for vanished youth;
we already had Perspective On Our Dreams . . .

Which made it, you see, all the more poignant
that this magical thing did seem to be happening tonight,
like in songs. Paralyzed
we sat and listened, silently agreeing to ignore the boredom
that was somehow necessary to the fine possibility.
The song that takes me back to David's dark room is "Ask Me
   Why"—
Richard sang along with it studiously, respectfully, as if to say
"This is indeed a profound text."
Lennon's voice so *authoritative* amid the light sweet lyrics:

   I can't believe
   it's happened to me
   I can't conceive
   of any more misery . . .

For some logistical reason, Richard and Ann
couldn't consider sleeping together that night,
and I think we were all glad—
why press the issue, let it be

■ 21

like Romeo and Juliet at the end of Act One,
safely lit up with anxious hope.

Next day Richard was hitchhiking to Boston, and Ann decided
to go with him. Ann wearing a gray jacket, Richard walking tall,
they got a ride right off the bat
and left Cathy and me waving from the sidewalk and feeling
strangely parental, proud and worried.
And I believe they lasted about a year.
Cathy and I lasted nearly two years altogether.
Ask me why,
I say I loved her, she loved me;
like a drug, or a dream, or a system of belief
while it lasted it was real.

BLIND DATE

My only blind date was arranged by Andy Effron.
We had been C.I.T.s together at Camp Mohawk
and Indian warriors together in the campfire ceremony
that came at the end of each camp session.
We laughed in the showers, trying
to get the red paint off
without enough hot water. Andy
thought life was hilarious and worthy of
energy—I liked him a lot—but
we were never really close friends—
it was an almost.

He was a year older. He was smart—
went to Harvard, made intriguing jokes
about the dirty Charles River
(I wasn't really sure what Boston was)
and in his free hours read *Situation Ethics.*
"Just do what seems right at any given time,
is that it?" "It's a little more
complicated than that," said Andy.
Meanwhile I was reading a private-eye novel;
Andy wondered why.
"I like its atmosphere," I said.

When I visited him at his family's house in Poughkeepsie
I enjoyed iced tea for the first time in my life.
We went bowling with that very muscular
swaggering guy whose real name was Richard
but who had some athletic nickname like Bo;
at Mohawk he had won the Talking Contest
by bellowing for four minutes straight.
I think I bowled terribly and felt like a wimp
but we drank beer and it became okay.

So, I thought, this is what it's like
to be a real American teenager—
I don't know, there was something so fifties
about it all—beer, bowling, swearing—
and then Andy getting me a blind date.
"She's not great to look at,
I'll be honest with you, but she's got
a great body and she's really
fun to be with."

She *was* nice. But I cherished
our mutual ignorance, and I think she did too:
it was what made us safe; we were adolescents,
sex proposed itself as the maddening center of life
and shallowness looked like the only peace.
Still I think she would have liked
a few kisses, at least; but I kept
my hands off her in the back seat—I was
polite—I could tell she thought I was
"cute" and probably "real sweet". The four of us
in Andy's green car (he had some funny name for it),
just out, in Andy's green car. . . . Driving
and burgers and a bar full of yelling jokers;
a few times Andy gave me a quiet look:
"For now, this is all we've got."
I thought about my blind date's body and how
the beer might make me bold, and there was nothing to lose . . .
But—I decided to let life
roll me on past these nights
toward some safety of *not needing* far beyond seventeen;
and felt the summer air
whip thru my fingers as Andy accelerated.

He was a smart guy. He did all these things
and still he was smart. He drank so much at the bar
twice he had to pull off the road to urinate.

We took his girlfriend home first
and his goodnight to her lasted twenty minutes. Obligatory.
Meanwhile I probably said something about
the Beatles to my date whose name
may have been Diane.

After we dropped off Diane, who said
it was nice to meet me,
we drove around, Andy and I,
I was thinking maybe Diane feels
great respect for me because I didn't
go after her breasts—and we drove
to Vassar, and toured the dark campus,
thinking of awesome girls in fragrant rooms;
then I didn't say, "We're on a blind date with life."
And on the radio came the Beach Boys
singing "Wouldn't it be nice if we were older
and we wouldn't have to wait so long."

Andy, this was supposed to be a sad story;
but I feel good, in the classic way,
having written it, and thinking of
what you might say now about summer nights
and the atmosphere of some only partly ethical situation.

VENUS PANDEMOS

What am I going to do with my desire
for women?

To be more specific, what am I going to do
with my interest in women's bodies?
Women's bodies—some—are so
terrific.
Every day—on the streets—

how should I feel about my lust?
Is it lust? "Lust" seems
such a fierce hairy word, I don't think
it quite applies. But there is this
energy—
I am a little excited just to describe it—
the quick expert evaluation of
face
breasts
ass
and then the instant summary judgment:
    "I crave her"
    "I'd take her"
    "Maybe if I was a little drunk and she threw herself on me"
or, more often:
    "Forget it, honey."

Breasts: why should they matter?
How dumb am I? Do I belong with
Hugh Hefner's legions of Total Assholes?
The word "breast" makes me queasy;
I wish it were spelled without the "a";
somehow the way it looks like a rhyme for "yeast"
is unsettling, and the way it somehow

reminds me of "roast". . . . Roast breast of turkey . . .
In my fantasies they are indeed a kind of food—
oh this is embarrassing. They *don't* have to be big;
if other aspects are fabulous, they can even be
quite small; but on strangers they do have to be
definite. Why?
To help make her manifestly Other.
Why? Hey, I don't know! Do I have to explain
everything? . . . Maybe the more Other she is
the less I feel obliged to treat her as a
fellow human. There, I said it, okay?

If a woman is walking toward me
and she gets a good rating for face and breasts
I turn, after she has passed,
to estimate the buttocks.
"Ass" seems such a nasty word,
perhaps antagonistic, certainly crass—
I never use it in conversation—
yet it is the word in my mind when
I turn on the sidewalk to glance back
and judge.

I wonder if any intelligent feminists
will ever read this poem.
I hope so; though the prospect makes me tense.
I wonder how much I have damned myself.
Not too much? "He's just another guy.
Just another sexist guy."
But that would be glib;
maybe most intelligent feminist readers would simply say
"shallow, horny, and exhibitionistic."
Would they say "adolescent"?
But that would be off-target since I'm sure I'm not unlike
plenty of men in their thirties, forties, fifties. . . .

"Ass" . . . Why this word?
Because it is so vigorous—so *direct*—
like a penis shoving home?
"Home"—what deep male need is revealed here?
Home to the Mother? I don't claim to know; but
I don't think so.
"Ass" . . . "Shoving home"—the fantasy here
is of seizing the woman's buttocks, *holding* them and
entering her vagina from behind;
why from behind? Bestial mastery. I guess.
Except that's not what I was going to talk about,
it could be from the front too as long as her
maddening ass is somehow under control, but to shove
"home" means all the way—
to her center—to
the place where it would not be possible
to *have* her any more than this.
"Have." "Possess." Oh, God.
What sick nexus of sexism and capitalism,
its hour come round again as usual,
rises banally and vilely to the light?

"Under control"—what is control?
"Possess"—but no, it isn't to possess.
I don't want such-and-such a redhead
the way I want new books, new records.
What about "conquest"?
Okay, maybe. Prove self's power with trophies,
"I had her, and her, and her," et cetera . . .
And yet: the energy I'm talking about
doesn't aim for anything so grandiose and arrogant as conquest.
No, it's
to do something about
her beauty.

To *do* something about her *beauty*!

Is it a defining quality of beauty
that it won't leave us alone?

When I see an especially attractive woman
something incredulous in me is suddenly convinced
that you can't just walk by,
you can't just glance at that signal,
that belling
without *responding;* to ignore it
would be death-in-life. . . .
What is to be done?
I've almost entirely outgrown—or,
given up—my fantasies of introducing myself
to strange women ("Excuse me,
I couldn't help noticing you're really beautiful,
I wonder if you'd like to have coffee with me?"),
and of course what I'm talking about
has nothing to do with rape. (Nothing?)
So I'm left to rely on my technique of
covert ogling-in-passing—
I eat them with my eyes.
—Is it like eating? It's a job of
disposing of them, one by one:

> *All right, I see that body,*
> *I have seen it.*

—Which means, that body is taken care of now,
that body is disarmed, normalized,
brought under control, it is forgivable now:
I have disposed of it through ritual,
the ritual of snapshot glancing, and now
its power is dead.
Ah. So is it, then, a kind of murder fantasy?
Jesus Christ. The penis shoving home
is the war machine blitzing all the way

to the citadel, and planting my flag.
Is that right? A spearing . . .
Like when I screamed at the other kids in war games
I GOT YOU! I got you now, honey,
you can't wriggle off. . . .
So am I saying that my ritual glancing
cannot be distinguished from phallic ambitions?
And "visual rape" is not a meaningless phrase?
Yes. I guess that's what I'm saying.
—But it's your fault, baby,
for being so GOD DAMN BEAUTIFUL.

Why am I saying all this?
Because what to do with this
energy
is a mystery: every day
I think about strange women, for quick seconds,
in ways which I consider dehumanizing.
Should I be ashamed?
I suspect my sexual fantasies are
among the tamest (most repressed?) anywhere;
and I can claim that my relations with the women I know
are relatively
nonsexist . . .
                    Oh I wish I could say
that beautiful women are no big deal!
But—like today, this high school girl
(I figure if she's under 18
I can call her a girl—I think)
who runs the tennis courts at Newton North:
the green eyes
the dark skin
the black hair
the green eyes glowing there
in her unexpectedly dark face

the healthy hardness of her bare thighs
the sudden clear smile at me
when I sign up for a court—
God!
I feel I should DO SOMETHING!

Since this is a problem *imposed* on me by beauty,
you can't call it mere "horniness."
And I can't cite loneliness as an extenuating circumstance—
I'm not lonely;
as it happens,
(—"as it happens": as I have made it happen,
partly in order to escape the tension and folly of hunting)
I live with a woman I love a lot.
I'm really not on the prowl for sex. Not literally . . .

> *I'm just a fella*
> *marooned on a sea of dames.*
I'm just a schnook who has to look.
I'm the guy

who sat around with my buddies Trey and Jon
in ninth grade and tenth singing along with
the Beach Boys et al. to give a shape to
our fervent quenchless ADMIRATION
for girls, girls galore.
We got doped up with some juice then
that fizzes every damn time we see or even hear about
"the healthy hardness of her bare thighs . . ."
It refuses to leave our veins (sometimes we honestly want it to).
My father at 65 is openly an ogler—
so I can't be expected to outgrow this
> *watchin'* all the girls
> *watchin'*
> *watchin'* . . .

■ 31

In 1973 and '74 I worked in a feminist theater group;
my awareness of the women's anger reached the point where
it seemed a crime for men to whistle at women on the street.
Now I'm not going to say it isn't.
But I'm admitting to an enduring energy in me that says
an attractive woman is not simply one more comrade on earth,
nor is she just another nice thing about life;

an ATTRACTIVE WOMAN is a PROBLEM.

And that's why
I've said all this:
bring your problems out into the open, it's
supposed to be healthy . . .
And I feel a little better; but not relaxed.

WHY THE HG IS HOLY

The Holy Ghost was browsing in his or her library
one day in the future, unaccountably bored,
oddly querulous, vaguely wanting something that would be
quietly unfamiliar. "It doesn't have to be *great*,"
said the Holy Ghost with the faintest note of exasperation
in his or her voice, "just so long as it has
its own special character."
Gliding along the billion shelves,
incredibly graceful despite his or her mood.
Then the deft and lovely hand of the Holy Ghost lit
on a slim volume of poetry—
it was your book.
It was your book.
The first poem caused the Holy Ghost to frown;
ah, but not with disdain, rather with curiosity!
The second poem brought a brightening of divine eyes.
And the page was turned as if by a pensive breeze.
Maybe it happened after your death, but so what? It
happened.
"I'm taking this back to my perfect desk,"
said the HG. "This is really something."

DESCRIBERS

Susan Sontag is down in New York City tonight
writing
and she wants to explain something to you.
She has it sort of figured out, or
part of it,
and she would like to set it straight for you.
William Gass is out in St. Louis
thinking
and he has a series of connections
between important ideas
which he'd like you to observe, and soon.
Have you got time?
He thinks you should make time.
At the offices of *Rolling Stone*
several young arbiters of pop culture
believe they have some rather startling insights
into the whole entire scene, you know,
and where it's going, and you could do worse
than to latch on to what they're saying.
One of the small-minded columnists
for our local daily paper
had an unusual experience last week
at the football stadium, or City Hall,
and he's all set to describe it to you.
He really *wants* to describe it,
describe it to you,
and in this instance there is actually
a kernel of true originality in his particular
angle of approach to the thing he saw—
it might be worth listening to!
Do you like clean water?
Of course you do—Ralph Nader
and his assistants are anxious to convey to you

quite a number of facts about clean water
and its future unavailability;
it's no use pretending you're not concerned
with clean water, you *must* be,
are you going to look up the Nader report
or not?
There's Robert Coles with plenty of
descriptions
of poor children, poor children there
and poor children there and there
and somewhere else—he is said to be
the best describer of the lives of poor children
currently describing them—you care
about poor kids, don't you? Yes:
you are decent.
Say, have you picked up the recent issue of
Ploughshares? I mean the fiction issue with
the story "El Paso" by Jayne Anne Phillips—
you didn't read that? Where have you been?
Just wait till you plunge into that small bitter world
described by Jayne Anne Phillips—
"scratch-clink of those claws against the boiling pots"—
she describes that world so you can't escape it.
I don't say that it's the best fiction around
but it is one thing and it is offered,
you say it's not *your* reality but
how insulated do you want to be?
Hold on, here's the new *New York Review*—
now don't give me that line about how
the *NYR* and all its competitors peddle nothing
but a rarefied brand of confusion based on
defensive obfuscation and frantic academic competition. . . .
Even if there's a smattering of truth in your charge
you know there's always *one* article that truly *needs*
to be read, one that will induce a recrystallization
of your thoughts about a First-Magnitude Problem.

■ 35

For example,—
but have you looked at *Ploughshares*?
Here, take my copy, take it, take it.
Jayne Anne Phillips is going to die—someday—
and she knows it—which is why
she wants you to take her El Paso
and keep it for her, somewhere—
have you got a safety-deposit box?
But back to the *New York Review*, sorry—
one gets deflected sometimes by alternative descriptions;
but I think you did acknowledge that there is always
at least *one* thing in the *NYR* for you.

Admittedly, these are mainly only
descriptions of descriptions. For example—
you know, so-and-so on Sartre's Genet—but
where did I put the new issue did you see where I
did I give it to you? No? Wait
maybe it's under this stuff. Oh Jesus . . . *Look*
at this *desk*! You know what those things are?
Descriptions!
The world is this, the world is that!
This aspect is actually a result of *that*
this of *that* insofar as *this*
whatever! Whatever. Holy shit
we can't stand it, can we? I mean can we
get on top of these? But what does
get on top mean, it means absorb, right?
But what if every new description renders the last one
untenable—*then* what, brainchild?
All these articulate god-damned descriptions
there is no *way* they could all be telling the "truth"!
. . . I'm sorry. Got a little excited. (I was
just trying to describe this feeling—
looking at this desk . . .)
Immature of me, I know—because

there's no doing without descriptions:
you *have* to want descriptions of reality:
because you don't ever get *reality.*
You get descriptions (d's).
D's are all we've got.

That's an idea. Wait a minute, now, that's
something we better think about—it's
the Borges idea, you know.
It's *The Sound and the Fury,*
it's *The Ring and the Book,*
The Turn of the Screw The Good Soldier
The Waves and you name the others,
d's of reality-as-tissue-of-d's—
and the idea that what we "know"
is only the d's we have fed ourselves. . . .

If that's how it is then
how can we choose one describer over another?
It's a free country, everybody has a right to describe
and there's no standard against which
to measure their failures:
how dare we ignore *any* voice?
—And yet—wait—isn't there something—
isn't there still the way we feel?
The way we really feel! That's
something, right?
If we can't call it truth because it's so wordless,
or not wordless but so muddy,
so tangled and shady and private, still
it is there. . . . And sometimes
a describer will, by some improbable maneuver,
weaving like Gale Sayers thru a storm of veteran formulas,
hit it: will say what limns the mapless airborne
all-but-ineffable gleamy crystal contours of
the way we feel!

Like Virginia Woolf when she wrote this:

There is a sound like the knocking of railway trucks in a siding. That is the happy concatenation of one event following another in our lives. Knock, knock, knock. Must, must, must. Must go, must sleep, must wake, must get up—sober, merciful word which we pretend to revile, which we press tight to our hearts, without which we should be undone. How we worship that sound like the knocking together of trucks in a siding!

Three years ago I read that and I said That's it! That's it!
She's got it!
                 —And then for a minute
everything is different: Language and
Truth
make eye contact and reflect each other
with rapt fidelity till you turn the page.
. . . But with our lives like Opening Day at the World's Fair
we can't always feel how we feel,
we feel a plagiarized version of our true thoughts
and con artists grab our coins and attention
as we wander reading
to the next and the next loud pavilion.

But. You keep trying. And they keep trying:
they push their d's at you and you read
and describe them to yourself and your friends
and your friends describe other d's to you
while new describers thrust new reams at you
like Jayne Anne Phillips who feels
that *you* might be her safety-deposit box.
You are WANTED by the describers.
They're not sure they're *real*
unless you pay attention. . . . If a d.
goes nowhere it feels as if it *came* from nowhere.

Thus the power you hold is great, and severe:

which way will you turn
in the deafening bookstores?
You are sought, Reader, you are infinitely sought!
You are the world's desire;
your unlooking can kill, your eyes decide
whom to verify, whom
to entomb.

It's no joke; you know that these people are
going to die. And they know it:
every little describer's body will die.
We ought to act accordingly. —Every day is
Keep Somebody Alive By Listening Day.
Listen, I know it's hard, advice is cheap
and mercy is expensive;
if you asked me in rush-hour traffic on a hot day
I would describe the poetry of Professor You-Know-Who as
"long-winded and flabby" but of course
it wouldn't be an adequate d. and
you would still be obliged to form your own d's
of his d's. . . . Listen,
there's a telegram for you at the desk
from Susan Sontag—go to it, go to it,
your switchboard is lit up like a Christmas tree.

—1979

THE STUDENTS

The students eat something and then watch the news,
a little, then go to sleep. When morning breaks in
they find they have not forgotten all: they recall
the speckle of words on certain pages of
the chapter assigned, a phrase of strange weight
from a chapter that was not assigned, and something
said almost flippantly by a classmate on the Green
which put much of the 18th century into perspective.
Noticing themselves at the sink they are aware
the hands they wash are the "same" hands
as in high school—though the face is different.
Arriving in the breakfast hall having hardly felt
the transit, they set down their trays on one table;
presently, glance at another corner of the space:
that was where we mostly sat two years ago,
that was where Gerry said what he said
about circles, the concept of, and Leonardo da Vinci.

WORK

Manual labor has barged into my life on many occasions
but seldom stayed long.
It's like an oafish cousin with thumping hands
who visits, always straining your hospitality,
his manners always cruder than you remembered,
then rumbles mercifully off toward some factory or ghetto.

When I worked for fourteen days in Gold's Delicatessen
just before my second year of college
I stole cheesecake in the cold storage room
even though Mr. Gold was an excellent man
who didn't have to give me this job but did so
as a favor to my mother who was a loyal
(but not wealthy) customer. I jammed my face
with cheesecake, nearly choked
trying to get it down before my absence could be noticed;
I strained my imagination trying to fully taste and enjoy
the cheesecake despite the speed of my chewing;
then, lips wiped on apron, back to the gray kitchen
to swab the echoing caverns of the pots
coated with corned-beef fat: swab gaily,
unbowed, because my mouth was coated
with gold, with the thrilling overtime pay of secrecy,
the taste of victory,
creamy sweetness of survival of the fittest,
Gold's expensive heavy New York–Style immortality.

Otherwise, on long days when no excuse took me
into the cold storage room, it was with death
those fatty vats resounded: nothing James Deany
but slow, glutinous, suburban drab death—

and I told myself *Beat this game,*
Dodge this ditch—
and something I called "the life of the spirit"
looked worth fighting for, scheming for:
make somebody pay me to read and write!
Mr. Gold was a good man but nothing he paid me
could have been enough, even for this
tolerable labor in a pleasant, proud deli:
if he had tripled my salary
maybe it would have been a few more weeks
before I started stealing, that's all.
. . . And eventually he'd have caught me
gorging the unearned sublime
and I'd have hated him for my shame.
And hated myself for being so clearly
an ant in an anthill and
unsatisfactory even at that.

Oh beat this game, dodge this ditch
I've coached myself year after year. . . .
"The dignity of labor" is a phrase that has always
troubled me—
isn't it mostly a negative definition of dignity?
I mean, it's dignity because of what it isn't:
if you're laboring you're *not* goofing off, *not* wasting time,
not running wild with desire. . . .
Then too, no doubt, something noble can be seen in
the concentration and diligence and steadiness with which
you scrub, tote, wrap, stack, count, dump, scrape.
Still such dignity doesn't clearly distinguish you
from the best of beavers or chimps, or even ants.

Leisure, now—that's a challenge.
Decadence knocks at the door and all the windows,
it softens the sofa.

Leisure says, "Are you here on earth *for* anything
except feeling swell?"
Sometimes I sit still for minutes upon minutes,
my hands doing nothing, vague noble mind seeking the cold
   vault
where waits the transcendental cheesecake of meaning.

HAPPINESS TIP

Your happiness contains the seeds of your sorrow;

you become aware of this recurrently,
in bitter absoluteness near the peak of sorrow
but also strangely on the rising slope of joy.
When the insight comes it need not be deathly
but it is guaranteed not to make you rapturous;
at best it can foster a philosophical peace,
an informed serenity, a sunset humor called "wry".

If it comes, somehow,
when your happiness is curving up toward a high,
or, more likely, toward an expected unlikely high,
you can hardly avoid feeling it as a qualm,
a spray of cold water, a shiver of death,
a hand of god pinching your shoulder
as if to say, "Quit acting up and sit down"
or "Have you done *all* your homework?"
There is bound to be a flicker of misgiving
when you get that flash about how
your happiness contains the seeds of your sorrow,

so you may as well accept it,
don't waste energy trying to ignore it—
besides, it's the truth, as far as we can tell,
and facing the truth, sooner or later,
seems necessary for leading a long fairly happy life
in the midst of such intractable reality.
So the smartest thing to do with the insight
is to take it as an insight, gracefully,
but not to let it swell up and smother you;
not to let it turn into a steel demolition ball
and bash down your frisky sweet-skinned burgeoning joy;

but just to nod at it, politely, give it the nod
as you lean out into your stride into the next good scene,
just nod as if to a glazed old gentleman on the corner
who periodically tells you the Governor's a crook
and whose heart coughs brown death at you
when you hesitate to hear some fragment
of the striving life that has dumped him at 68
into Social Security and spitting grief—
just give it the old nod, casual as you please,
and flip it right into your pocket,
let it sit quiet there next to your keys
for as long as you can leave it alone.
Let it take care of its own re-emergence,
all in time, it will manage to come out
all in time, time sooner or later
too late for any other thought
(but it too will pass, dissolve, wash away).
And in the meantime while you try to be happy,
which is sensible and strangely not automatic,
the insight will be down there quiet in your pocket,
there for you to caress it absently
from time to time, like an old coin.

WESTERN NORTH CAROLINA

Consider the annals of a small town
in western North Carolina. Assemble
the interesting sequences of fact and supposition
from several points of view. Sift.

Beyond a certain point, you say,
these facts are not interesting; or,
you say you'll never be able to uncover
details vivid enough to be interesting.
You are wrong on both counts. Or,
I tell you now to assume
that you are wrong on both counts.
Assume the facts about this town are
interesting; make them interesting.

Pick a town with which you have no tie:
no distant relative, no friend
whose wife or father grew up there.
Pick a town that means zilch in your book;
build an extra chapter.

Trace marriages and divorces,
illegitimate births and abortions—
talk to all the doctors. Listen to
the old women who think you're strange,
find how to soften their distrust,
go back to them again and again,
make them see open interest in your eyes.
And the oldest man, dabbling at his tomato soup
on the porch of the Oddfellows Home—
get past his shell of taciturnity,
lead him into long rants and tales,
bring him some Juicy Fruit gum

and pictures of Marilyn Monroe or John Wayne
and ask again about love and grief in the town
and try hard to get all the names.

Later, go back to the town in another season.
Visit the spots where certain couples cried or kissed
in snow or summer dust. Stand there
feeling the air and recalling the names.
There are families on the north side
along by Thorpe Lake or Shooting Creek
that you haven't considered yet.
Consider them: widen your chapter
with new pages and weave them,
the Whitnels and Ashfords and Yadkins,
in among the Gilkeys and Buckners you have already
considered. Walk to the old high school
at dawn, from many different directions.
You won't finish, but that's no excuse for quitting.

Do all this because you too are obscure.
Do all this because it could have been you
screaming at your black-bearded father
and running down the back steps before he could
club you with his bottle of sour mash.
Do all this to create
the possibility
that someone somewhere could unpredictably
and without obvious selfish motive
care for your life.

When you want a vacation from your first adopted town,
you have many choices. To the west,
there is Crabtree that merits some attention,
and Dellwood, and farther south,
Tuckasegee.
The map of your conscience seems to have no borders.

One drop of sweat falls from your eyebrow
and lands in the Great Smokies.

You'd better rise and shine, you lonesome anthropologist,
you haven't got all day.

NEW YORK BREEZE

My father on a June night says "God, it's cool"
and I place an empty wineglass on the small yellow
table in the kitchen, in the dark; life seems
to go on as a series of experiences. Amazing
that this can feel like an insight. There is cool air
when you wouldn't expect, and a sense
that all the poems being written are tolerable,
and someone will seriously read
all the books brought out since 1972;
because there is not too much of anything exactly
but there is a great number of things
and living is to move through them one
by one. Now my father is wearing his white jeans
which are part of his present life which
has come after my mother's death and it's a sequence
of lives, isn't it, each with its own clothes
or the same shirts but they become old shirts
which are not the same as before—platitudes
revolve like undiscovered planets in my mental zodiac—
my father is fiddling with his new cassette tape deck,
bought on sale: Japanese technology seems
part of a vast system for helping us believe in
change: this is the possession of this latest
life. . . . My father studies the dials and
a New York breeze trembles the cover of O'Hara's
Lunch Poems (a present for Lisa). . . . What
was it one had to say? (Not only is it fun
to call myself "one" but it feels correct
at the moment because isn't everyone
involved in this elaborate okayness of sequence?)
My father gets Ginny and me to try the headphones
while he makes a tape of "Meditation Mama":
"Time don't mean a thing, 'cept that the world goes around . . ."

Oh, wisdom abounds, and is curiously unstartling!
One will continue living living for decades, placing
a given glass on a given table—a particular table
which for one second turns unforeseeably vivid:
the wooden tabletop stunningly yellow and thus
the blazing sun of this tiny landscape which includes
your dark self arrested in the black window
like a sea horse pausing underwater, what are you doing?
You are caught in a moment of silence in a narrow kitchen
beside this yellow table, caught caring about small things,
an empty glass, a book of matches, a greasy knife, and
your strangely unmomentous reflection. . . . And
back in the next room, when one's father
or daughter
offers thoughts on the new movie
one will raise one's eyebrows concernedly and say
"Is that right?"

COVER VERSIONS

At night I take the inner life
out of its sleeve, put on the headphones
and let it spin.
I know the grooves where the needle is liable to hang—
there's Mummy sobbing "But that's my boy" at Kennedy Airport,
there's Daddy saying "You can't just sit under a tree
and invite your soul."
There's Cathy crying "I'm not the same!"
and Eric, at the bottom of the stairs,
only saying "I thought we were friends."

There is one song on Side B the needle
never seems to get to.
I wake at night and through many floors
I can almost hear the bass guitar giving that song
a rock outline cut in the black dirt below me.
If I ever hear it, I'll know that tune—
ethereal harmonies like the Everly Brothers
at their best; Cathy sits beside me on the sofa,
Eric deigns to keep time, Daddy thinks I've done well
—all in that song—and my mother's sort of still alive.
Meanwhile
I haven't quit shopping for cover versions
that get a few things right.

SUNRISE AND THE BOMB

Sunrise

I've seen it so seldom, it has been mostly
just a concept to me, metaphor for improvement
or rejuvenation or whatever—
but this—
my God!
Scarlet shot with gold
and/or gold shot with scarlet!

Spreading! The power!

Over Boston, embracing sleepy worn Boston,
bespeaking something absurdly larger than Boston

how it reaches radiant
into and across
slowly but absolutely
the undarking awakening cloud-riffled
sky!

From this hill I can see
where Hopkins got his religion.
(And his diction, almost. What are you going to do
when you actually see
a sunrise? Use obvious words? That would seem a betrayal.
You'll go for "undarking" "blossomflood"
                "heavenblood" "wound-birth" . . .)

The earth is
turning! Eastward—
continents rushing with unforfeited dignity to meet
the sun—

such absolute assurance in the encounter—
infinite passion flower
(Lawrence would be pleased if he were here on the hill)
we could say the cosmos is making love to itself
where the earthly meets the glory of the sky. . . .
We could talk all morning about sunrise
and not say it.

Notice, though, that I'm not saying
"hope" and "renewal" and "endless life"
much less "God's grandeur"
much less "God's love"—

before dawn I was thinking about nuclear war
the proliferation of nuclear weapons
the existence of the silos and Polaris submarines
I believe they are not only words and photos in magazines
I believe they are physical facts;
when was the last time mankind was capable of
a vast act of intelligent forbearance from obvious folly?
Do you know? And how long did it last?

Like fire, like blood, the huge event in the east is
beautiful; it is so big that human doom looks small
and I stand on my little hill thinking, "Well, we tried"
and imagining some beings a thousand years hence
who uncover our leavings

and they find, for instance,
the LP by Tom Waits called *Closing Time*
and they listen to the first song,
"Ol' 55"—

the guy has had some trouble at a bar
someone doesn't love him much
and before dawn he finds himself

out on the highway in his ol' 55;
the song is filled with that sense of
being still alive when
it makes no sense to be still alive
the sun comes up over a cloverleaf intersection
where he can choose between roads to nothing
—the guy knows he has made a mess of it all
but he finds that he's still driving
and he stays well ahead of three trucks.

FUNCTIONAL POEM

Is there any reason why a poem shouldn't
at least occasionally
come through for us in a concrete way and
get something done?

Because I need to get something across
to a particular individual
with whom I have no normal contact,
I mean I never see this guy, and yet
I've got something to say to him—
and me being a poet I naturally
have to use
the means at my disposal.

The individual to whom I refer
is a young man with blond hair,
I admit from a certain point of view
many people would consider him handsome although
he's what I call rather heavy-set i.e.
chubby. Well-dressed, the guy has money, I'm sure
he wears those yellow-white cotton pants
made for people like golfers and princes
who can take everything slow and cool—
not that he does. Because

the one time I saw this guy
on a hot inter-suburban street some years ago
he was driving his white Camaro
with his radio on terrifically loud with
some old Beach Boys song which I normally like
but it seemed a sacrilege for this rich guy to have
that old gentle lighthearted music in his Camaro—
the song was a hit when this character was about

five years old, for god's sake!—
but anyway he cuts right in front of me,
I'm driving my father's old VW,
he almost clips my fender, gives me this look,
like "You're over the hill, man, get off the road"—
I'm under 35 and this guy is telling me
I'm over the hill! So naturally
I give him a blast on the horn.
So then the bastard slows way way down.
So I pass him, except all of a sudden
he speeds up to keep even with me,
I'm stuck out in the left lane
and here comes a frigging truck or something!
So I hit the brakes and duck in behind him
in his beautiful creamy white Camaro
with the Beach Boys and a little cooler of
Miller High Life in the back seat, I'm sure.
Almost immediately he does the slow-down thing again—

and this time he lets me pass him.
But then about thirty seconds later
vrrrroooooommm!—he's passing me
but there's traffic coming toward us,
God, my heart seized up like a broken clutch—
but
he made it, the bastard,
I admit he had great acceleration,
and nerve, too, the guy had nerve—
he pulled away into the distance,
going even faster to show me that
the near-miss never scared him for a second.

Okay. Now, I've thought it over,
and I realize that what's wrong with this individual
is not that he's rich, or that he's young,
or that he's a little on the heavy side.

That stuff is his business, and the same goes
for the loud radio as far as I'm concerned and
the fast driving too, even, in most situations.
But what's wrong with the guy is
that he made me run the risk of
severe damage to life and limb or
possibly a fatality, i.e. I could have been killed.
And that is just not acceptable.
I'm saying, this person cannot be permitted
to do such a thing.

Now, I know all your theories, by the way,
about "Poetry makes nothing happen"
and art is not a tool or weapon et cetera.
But on the other hand it *is* a way of giving messages,
and if I'm being a little more honest about this
than most poets, then so be it;
and I'm just giving that blond individual
this message:

Don't go around interfering with somebody else's
right to live, you stupid jerk.
Why don't you consider some other life-style
less dangerous to others and yourself as well?
Why don't you read some poetry once in a while?
If this poem can do a job on you,
maybe others can, too. Why don't you
take some of your gas money and
subscribe to a few poetry magazines?
Think about it.

Readers, if you see the above individual,
or somebody like him, could you
please just pass along this message.

LITTLE STAR

"Stop here, or gently pass!"
—WORDSWORTH

I

"Little Star" by the Elegants (1958)
is one of those perfect early rock/pop songs
that radiate confidence in a few
orderly truths. Above all,
if you have the right girl as your girlfriend—
you know, the one who walks that way
and tosses her hair, the one who dances
just a little between cheers at the football game—
if you've got her, you're golden,
there's nothing else you could wish for.
Oh, God, do you remember the golden liquidity
of the lead singer's voice
as he expresses this shapely truth—
he could get it across without needing to rely
on the mere meanings of words—
he could do everything with golden syllables!

Who was he?
Can anybody tell me the name
of the lead singer for the Elegants?
In view of that grand confidence
it would seem a name worth preserving.
Really—if you can give me his name
I'll give you six dollars.
(I thought of offering ten, but that seems
more than I can afford, especially since
his name may be fairly easy to discover;
five dollars nowadays seems paltry,
so I'm offering six.)

II

This is not the first time I've tried to
get a rock-&-roll song into a poem and it won't be
the last; it is my need to call out
This counts too!
I don't deny Homer, or Virgil, or Dante
I'll take your word for it about Bach and Beethoven
I don't question the importance of the Bible
though it never lived in my life,
I love Shakespeare and admire Milton as much
as you do, but our lives go on
in these years, 1958, 1959, 1960,
"the sixties", and still on in these years like
1977 and still on now, as I write this
in September 1980 with the sun bright
almost as if new—and we are small,
we are postmodern and small, but not therefore worthless;
so it is for our sake
that I try to insist upon the wafer-thin golden value
of a certain addition to the long, long,
overtalented symphony of culture.
Of course it's no match for some hundreds
or even thousands
of novels, poems, operas etc. we could name,
nor for fifty rock songs I could name;
but I want to say
"This, also, was not nothing."

III

Where is he now?
The Elegants would be in their forties now.
Is he a vice-president of Arista Records?
Is he a wise quiet junkie on the Lower East Side?
Is he dead—killed by something that golden syllables

can't fix? Or maybe
at this moment he sits with another Elegant
in a Pizza Hut in L.A.,
planning the impossible comeback!

If you can let me know where he is
I'll send him a fan letter—
the unforeseeability of this gesture would make me feel,
at least for a day, that a million debts were paid.
However, the six dollars will be yours
for no information more than his name—
his name. The point
is just to make it true
that someone twenty-two years after a small
fact of art can unexpectedly pause and say,

This man sang lead on "Little Star".

A NOTE ABOUT THE AUTHOR

Mark Halliday's poems have appeared in *Ploughshares*, *The New Republic*, *Massachusetts Review*, and *Michigan Quarterly Review*. He has received a B.A. and an M.A. from Brown, and a Ph.D. from Brandeis. He was born in Ann Arbor, Michigan, and now lives in Philadelphia, where he teaches at the University of Pennsylvania.